INDEXED ANNUITY SECRETS

INDEXED ANNUITY SECRETS

How the Affluent Escape the 401(k) Trap to Exponentially Grow Their Wealth

GREGORY STEVENSON

Published by Best Seller Publishing®, St. Augustine, FL
Best Seller Publishing® is a registered trademark.
Printed in the United States of America.

ISBN: **978-1-962595-23-0**

This publication is designed to provide accurate and authoritative information with regard to the subject matter covered. It is sold with the understanding that the publisher is not engaged in rendering legal, accounting, or other professional advice. If legal advice or other expert assistance is required, the services of a competent professional should be sought. The opinions expressed by the author in this book are not endorsed by Best Seller Publishing® and are the sole responsibility of the author rendering the opinion.

For more information, please write:
Best Seller Publishing®
1775 US-1 #1070
St. Augustine, FL 32084
or call 1 (626) 765-9750
Visit us online at: www.BestSellerPublishing.org

Disclaimer

This is a work of nonfiction. All of the events in this collection are true to the best of the author's memory. Some names and identifying features may have been changed to protect the identity of certain parties.

This book discusses Fixed Indexed Annuities (FIAs) and related strategies. It is for informational purposes only and not a substitute for personalized advice. FIAs offer a guaranteed minimum return but are subject to caps, participation rates, and surrender charges. Past performance is not indicative of future results. Consult a licensed financial advisor and tax professional before acting.

Gregory Stevenson (CA License #4132743). FIAs may include surrender charges (e.g., 7-10% early withdrawal) and optional rider costs affecting returns.

Dedication

To Those Who Give an Opportunity and Example

Contact Information

Gregory Stevenson: +1 (619) 374-8100 (a text will work)
LinkedIn: Gregory Stevenson
Instagram: Gregory_Stevenson
Website: https://indexedannuitysecrets.com
For the one-page plan:
https://indexedannuitysecrets.com/one-page-plan

Table of Contents

Acknowledgments

I want to thank and acknowledge my mentors, business partners, and family who have played a huge role in the completion of this book.

I intend for this book to bring thousands of people a few steps closer to their goals and dreams. I will offer tools, history, examples, and education.

Faith, family, finance, fitness, and fun. It's truly what I believe every great culture should have: the five F's. I believe deep down in my core that everything I do should be done with integrity and sincerity.

This is why I'm devastated when I find people who have spent a lifetime serving others and still can't retire, moms who can't take care of their families, or dads who always worked long hours and never planned properly.

I looked into my industry, the wealth management space, and I saw so many people being overlooked and underserved.

I'm tired of people getting taken advantage of by Wall Street and their many lies. I will shed light in this area and provide a glimmer of hope in a sea of doubt. Many people will use this book, so I hope you will share it.

Introduction

BOTTOM LINE UP FRONT

❝ In this book I will share information about something called an *indexed annuity*. This vehicle has no fees, absolutely no downside risk, and market-like returns. ❞

This book will reveal what an *indexed annuity* is and what it can do for you and your family. I will speak in simple, easy-to-understand terms that will help you achieve your financial dreams, goals, and aspirations.

At the end of this book, you will have enough information to decide if indexed annuities are right for you.

As you read through this book, you may feel this program is too good to be true. Trust me, everyone does until they learn the truth behind this secret. Give us an hour and 20 minutes to read this book, and I will give you everything you need to know about the best-kept secret in the financial industry.

Indexed annuities are a powerful yet often overlooked option in financial planning.

Typically, they have no explicit management fees, but surrender charges or optional rider costs may apply. They offer principal protection, subject to caps and participation rates.

About the Author

With many years of experience managing millions in assets, having hundreds of personal clients alongside thousands of licensed professionals in his industry, Gregory has a book you must read. He has a deep understanding of indexed annuities and the solution they bring.

Gregory is highly qualified to teach this financial tool. His strategies go beyond conventional advice, focusing on stable growth and risk management. In certain scenarios, they can even outperform traditional advisors and IRAs over any ten-year period.

He adapts to economic shifts, ensuring security and peace of mind for his many clients—a level of expertise you won't find elsewhere.

A Message to the Reader

I wrote this book simply because there is not a single authority in this space on indexed annuities that I could point to. I believe it's because of the nature of these products. Once you get one, you won't want anything else. As a result, advisors won't offer it until it's the last stop. I find there is not a single person that I can point to who is true north. Someone who does the right thing and gives the full account of information and education for people to make the best decision.

Time and time again, I would fail to point my clients towards a resource that they could read and have all the resources to make a decision. I believe that I should be the difference I wish to see in this world.

PART I
THE HISTORY

Chapter 1

History Wasn't
Always This Way

Take a walk with me in history and take a moment to picture this: it's 180 A.D. You've lived a simple life in the Roman Empire. You live in a region called Tyre (or modern-day Lebanon), tending to your fields, helping local townspeople thrive, as a dedicated farmer for over 30 years.

You have a happy and healthy family, and you've lived a fulfilling life. You've worked hard and paid your taxes. At the end of your career, you hear about an offer. In exchange for making a single payment to a financial institution, you will receive annual payments for the remainder of your life. You can now live worry-free towards this last chapter of your life. This was a deal so attractive even some local Egyptians deemed it fit for their princes. A lot simpler than today, you would imagine.

Fast forward 1600 years to 1759, a time before the birth of the United States of America, during an era of British colonization. The Pennsylvanian Presbyterian ministers had a very important role in Colonial America, even contributing to the revolutionary movement by undermining the authority of colonial rule. During this time, ministers would make a single payment towards the church and would use the same tool that the ancient Romans used to provide a stream of income. If they were to become sick, ailing, or die, it would give income to their families for a lifetime of dedicated work serving in the church. The same ministry even loaned $5,000 (modern-day $210,000) to help finance Revolutionary War efforts.

Fast forward yet again, bringing us to October 1929, the stock market crash, a time that's considered devastating and full of loss. The sudden plummet of 22% happening in such a short amount of time was just the opening act for the next few years to come.

People sought out more reliable investments in order to safeguard themselves from financial ruin. With the economy less stable than it had ever been, many individuals looked for a haven of stability in what seemed a sea of doubt. During that time of hardship in 1929, the same vehicle that provided those with clarity is now viewed as a safe haven for your money to this day. Americans who wanted to protect their savings against the Great Depression had to get smart. The market had no other safe choice.

Studying century by century can seem like a long time, and it is. But history must be studied to not make the same mistakes. What I have found in my search is this ancient secret that existed from the Roman Empire, surviving during the Revolutionary War, giving clarity during major market crashes, to saving retirement in modern-day America. This secret has been in front of us the whole time.

It has provided peace of mind to millions of people, protecting their future, creating stability, and helping solve the age-old question:

When can I retire?

Same Rules, Different Name

In Rome, it was called Annua.

In Colonial America, it was called a fixed annuity.

In 1929, American investors called it "depression proof."

Modern-day affluent investors call it an indexed annuity.

I like to call it the best thing since sliced bread, but realistically it predates sliced bread.

Famous People who Invested in Annuities

When I started to study further than my knowledge as a licensed financial professional, I didn't expect to discover how popular annuities have been through history. A few of the famous people in history who have used this program to build wealth include Albert Einstein, Babe Ruth, and Benjamin Franklin, just to name a few.

Albert Einstein the scientist, invested wisely in annuity funds as part of his strategy to ensure financial stability for himself and his family, even going as far as calling compound interest "the greatest mathematical discovery of all time."

Babe Ruth the baseball player was also a savvy investor. Aware of the unpredictable nature of a sports career, Ruth wisely diversified his income streams; he invested in annuities to secure his financial future.

Benjamin Franklin was a founder of our country and an inventor. In his autobiography, Benjamin Franklin famously shared his wisdom on the subject of financial planning. One of his enduring quotes, "An investment in knowledge pays the best interest," still resonates today. Franklin's approach to finance extended to his own life, as he was known to have invested in annuities as a means of securing a steady income for his retirement years.

Chapter 2

Betty, Rob, History, and the Billions of 401(k) Fees

Let's address the elephant in the room in this chapter: 401(k) fees.

Do you remember getting your first job? What an amazing milestone that was! Everyone was so proud to watch you become the adult you dreamed of, get the position you longed for, and put in the extra effort to get.

Before you knew it, you were told to quickly sign some paperwork for a 401(k) and be off to the races, nothing to dwell on. You had to get to work, start paying your bills, take care of your family, and eventually retire as the adult you were expected to be.

The 401(k), the retirement vehicle that we are supposed to use and magically retire with one day, right? That's what I was told growing up, and those around me seemed to agree. Everything is supposed to be this way, and it all just makes sense. Doesn't it? You work a job, find a nice career, and get the benefits at 65 (if you even make it that far). You get to travel the world, and everything will work out. Sure! Have you ever taken a moment and asked those around you or asked those already at age 50, 55, or even 60 how retirement looks?

Surely we can find people in our lives that have used the 401(k) for retirement. They must be very excited!

Sweet Betty

Let's introduce Betty. Betty is a baby boomer born in 1960. She is a 64-year-old nurse who lives in the state of Indiana at the time of this writing in 2024. She was the sweetest woman when I met her. She even offered to make me and my wife a pie. She is an all-American woman, full of energy and dreams. She has raised two young men whom she is proud of. They have both grown up and become independent, now living in California and Florida. Her son Ethan, who I attend church with, introduced me to her.

As I learned Betty's story, I became deeply distressed because of the advice she told me she had been receiving. She always had a solid career and trusted what her job said when it came to getting the 401(k) match. She said it was like getting free money, but the job never offered any advice with that free money or where to invest it. Betty did retire at the age of 60 on January 1, 2020. She retired not knowing her full retirement age (the age needed to collect Social Security). She withdrew her money out of her company's 401(k) and took it to a financial advisor in the year she retired. She wanted the money placed into the stock market to be managed.

She figured all she had to do was get to the magical age of 60. On March 23, she had the shock of her life. That very same year she was forced back into her work due to her 401(k) suffering an almost 32% loss! Alongside this, she ended up pulling $130,000 out for retirement in 2020, which resulted in Betty paying $36,072 in taxes to keep her standard of living.

Source Investopedia https://indexedannuitysecrets.com/active-resources

Source CNBC https://indexedannuitysecrets.com/active-resources

While she was investing into a 401(k), she'd always assumed taxes would be lower later in life. She'd guessed they wouldn't be so much of a burden. She figured it would all be taken care of. It might be easy to brush Betty's story off, but Betty is one of the reasons I'm writing this book. Let's keep in mind that most people are not aware that when you receive the match on your 401(k), you pay the taxes on the money they match you later.

Let me say that again. The money they match you is not free; you pay the taxes on the match later when you pull it out. You're also paying fees on the money they give you. That means the more money the company contributes, the more taxes and fees you will pay. At the same time, the company gets a tax deduction in the year they contribute.

I will discuss this in later chapters.

I met Betty in January 2023 after she said she had enough of the games with retirement. Betty listened to a friend and placed her IRA into the S&P 500 in 2022 after realizing she didn't want to work anymore as she approached the age of 65. She wanted to hurry up and make some money because she didn't have enough to last her in retirement at that point.

She simultaneously sought out her advisor who told her there were not many options available other than keeping it under management. After entering the market again with that advice, Betty lost another 22.9% in 2022.

Source Investopedia https://indexedannuitysecrets.com/active-resources

Source CNBC https://indexedannuitysecrets.com/active-resources

I asked if her friend that recommended the S&P 500 had a license to offer advice; she shrugged and said she didn't know. When I asked Betty her concerns and reasons for seeking better advice, they were as follows:

Why do I have to work past 65?

Why am I not any good at this?

How am I supposed to retire with this?

What will my kids do if I can't afford retirement?

Why didn't anyone teach me what this would look like later in life?

I will come back to Betty.

Betty's story is not uncommon. Many people I've met over the years have felt the same way.

They don't understand retirement. They don't have any real advice near them and are simply doing what they are told by society and Wall Street advice. Why did Betty even invest in the 401(k) in the first place? Where did the 401(k) plan come from, and how did it become so prevalent in our society in such a short amount of time? Keep in mind the 401(k) was created in 1978, less than 50 years old at the time of this book.

Classy Rob

Let's introduce another one of my clients, Classy Rob. Rob is 58. He grew up in San Diego, California. He's got a killer mustache and always has a smile and laugh to share. He has the funniest things to say. He's a real classy guy; when we went out to dinner he always held the door open and even offered to pay the bill. I wouldn't allow it. My wife and I are the ones helping Rob. Not the other way around.

In 2014, Rob went to a financial advisor at age 48 with $300,000 after leaving his 30-year career. His money was placed into a variable annuity.

At first, it seemed great, until the 2020 market crash. Three years later, he had lost around $200,000 in fees and market loss, essentially placing him right back where he started. If he had selected an indexed annuity in 2014, based on historical averages, he could have had closer to $600,000 in 2022. He lost this money even though his advisor offers an indexed annuity! Imagine being so close to the solution, but the person helping you won't take the time to explain it.

When I asked the advisor why he offers indexed annuities (which I knew he did because I looked up his product list on his company's website), but he wouldn't offer Rob the indexed annuity, the advisor paused for a moment and then finally said it wouldn't perform the same.

He didn't elaborate any further and offered no other advice. It was as if he was coached to say that. The truth is, he wouldn't get paid the 1% - 2% a year to manage the money. Bad financial advisors are less worried about growing your actual wealth than they are about managing your 1% - 2% every year. After four months of going back and forth, I finally helped Rob and got him a tax-free bucket on his portfolio.

Check in later chapters for the results.

I want to invite you to answer these same questions.

Do you know what a 401(k) is?

Do you know how your 401(k) works?

Do you know the major rules of your 401(k)?

Do you know how the 401(k) will achieve your goals?

I ask these questions and hardly get any good responses. I'm no longer surprised when someone who has been working at the same company for ten or twenty years replies with no to one or all of these questions. Here is the truth. Chances are you simply got it because your job offered it to you, **not because someone educated you on it** or because it was the right vehicle for you, **but simply because it was offered.**

Bad Advice

The 401(k) has benefits, but in my experience throughout the years as a financial professional I have watched as many good people have continuously failed to hit their goals while saving in retirement through a company 401(k). Taxes, market loss, and fees are three reasons I often have to redirect people's plans.

As I look at the current generation that should be retired all across the United States, I find myself walking into grocery stores or gas stations, and I see people who are well into their late 60s or 70s still working. They should be retired, but they are not. My point here is that poor planning plus the 401(k), combined with predators who take advantage of good people, has failed many. This statement also includes financial advisors who sit by and do a poor job with assets under management, do the absolute bare minimum, and offer little to no advice. I hope that you'll join me in this journey of reading our book, understanding how indexed annuities work, the promises they keep that have been around for centuries, and how it will truly save you and the millions of people that it has helped. Keep in mind LIMRA (a trade association serving the financial industry) reports in 2023 385.4 billion in annuity sales. This information is no secret to the affluent; only to those who need it.

Source Limra *https://indexedannuitysecrets.com/active-resources*

Chapter 3

Why the Affluent Avoid the 401(k) Risk

The first failure is the ability to lose net worth at the whim of Wall Street. The ups and downs of the stock market can have a significant impact on your retirement. Many people saw their retirement savings plummet during 2000–2002, the 2008 recession, and the most recent economic downturn caused by the COVID-19 pandemic. While the stock market may eventually bounce back, the affluent don't play the "dumb risk" game. They don't have to.

It can take years to recover from these losses, if at all.

Lawsuits

Additionally, 401(k)s have some protection, but annuities may offer more, meaning your savings are exposed to lawsuits and other external factors that can significantly impact your retirement savings. You can lose your money. If your company is sued, pensions and 401(k)s can be impacted by lawsuits, which cost the sponsors a lot of money for legal fees, settlements, and judgments. These losses cause the amount of funds that are available for benefits and investments to diminish drastically. The effects even reach administrative practices and investment options. Not only that, but legal options can also attract examinations, audits, and fees. These changes in plans and legal actions can change the perspective, trust, and confidence of the participants.

The Hidden Flaws of the 401(k)

Advisor fees can cost around 1% to 2% a year on average. That means that in a $1M 401(k), it will cost you $10,000-$20,000 yearly—$200,000 over 20 years. Administrative and soft-dollar fees (buried in expense ratios) can hit 4%. NerdWallet estimates $590,000 lifetime losses. Most people don't even know they are paying it, or that they even have fees on their account! Take a $1,000,000 401(k)/IRA; 1% comes to $10,000 a year just for a lousy financial advisor to charge you and ignore you when the market crashes.

To make matters worse, it is standard practice not to offer a different product to you unless advisors can make money with management fees! They will even tease each other if they aren't able to close a product with management fees. For reference, in the example above, 20 years of management comes to $200,000 at 1%. Hidden fees are another drawback of the 401(k). Employers can pass on administrative, transfer, investments, and other fees to their employees. Another one is soft-dollar fees, which are fees passed alongside investments. Soft-dollar fees are very difficult to uncover because they are buried in a mutual fund's expense ratio.

In fact, the fees can add up to 4% a year. A 2019 study by Nerd-Wallet found that the average American could lose up to $590,000 in fees over the course of their lifetime due to 401(k) fees. These fees can be even higher for small companies that do not have the bargaining power to negotiate lower fees.

Source NerdWallet https://indexedannuitysecrets.com/active-resources

Limited Investment Options

401(k)s restrict you to mutual funds, risking over-concentration, which have been decimated in past crashes. This limitation can hinder potential investment growth and limited options by putting all your eggs in one basket. This lack of investment diversity can have terrible consequences. For example, many 401(k) accounts were decimated during the stock market crash of 2000 through 2002, 2008, and 2020 and 2022. These flaws in the 401(k) system have left many Americans with less-than-ideal savings for retirement, and it's time for a solution. (By the way, the fees in the 401(k) industry are a stand-alone **billion-dollar industry**.)

Source Investopedia https://indexedannuitysecrets.com/active-resources

Early Withdrawal Penalties

The next biggest failure is the limit on even being able to access money until the age of 59 and ½. If you do withdraw funds before age 59½, you will incur a 10% penalty plus taxes—20-35% federal, and 5-9% state tax. 80% of lower-income Americans face this scenario when they have an emergency. Let that sink in for a moment. Why should we ever be told to wait until a certain age to access our money? This rule still blows my mind to this day and even more so that we have been conditioned to believe this as normal. There are better ways to grow your money and avoid market loss while keeping it liquid.

The Early Withdrawal Penalties or EWP affect an expected 80% of lower-income Americans who access 401(k) early and pay EWPs due to avoiding loss of home or medical emergencies.

Source Vanguard/Insight https://indexedannuitysecrets.com/active-resources

In other words, you may lose 20 to 35% in federal taxes and 5 to 9% in state taxes, along with an additional 10% penalty, just to access your own money! This is why being educated is more important to the affluent than being sold, and many workers are sold a 401(k) for the company's benefit.

When people are diagnosed with a serious disease like cancer, heart attack, or another illness they have to take time off for medical treatment. After enough time off work, they will be fired from their job. It's simple. This is because they are not working the hours they need to and the company can only be so nice before they let you go. Generally, people in this situation don't sell their family home. Instead, they'd rather liquidate and pull out of retirement early, which means paying these high taxes and penalties. Unfortunately, this is not an if but a when for many Americans; it's just the math of the situation.

Let's not forget the taxes. Ask yourself whether taxes are going up or down? How many years are you from retirement? Is it worth losing money and paying high taxes?

Required Minimum Distributions

Next, the Requirement of Minimum Distributions (RMDs) states that at the age of 73 years old, those individuals are forced by the government to withdraw a certain amount from their 401(k)s, whether they need it or not. This results in an excise tax of 50% if you don't pull out funds! Keep in mind the government can change the age of your RMD rule at any given moment.

Source IRS https://indexedannuitysecrets.com/active-resources

But they still invest Having too much money in a 401(k) can actually hurt you in later years. All these factors combined have made the 401(k) an unreliable and inadequate retirement vehicle for many Americans. **But they still invest**. The affluent simply avoid these plans because once you learn what is available to you outside of the company 401(k), financial freedom becomes that much closer. So, what is the alternative to the 401(k)? In the following chapters, I will introduce you to a better solution for your retirement savings – indexed annuities.

So far in this book, I have covered history, flaws, and culture and why the affluent don't play "dumb risk." In the next chapters, I will give you tools, actual results, live accounts, and stories of those I have served and helped.

PART II
THE SHIFT

Chapter 4

The Shift from the Pension

Let's start with the basics. What is a 401(k), and how does it work? A 401(k) is a retirement plan offered by a company where you contribute a portion of your salary towards your retirement savings. This amount is then invested in stocks, bonds, or mutual funds, with the hope that your money will grow over time. Does hope sound like a good strategy? The contributed amount is not taxed until it is withdrawn, usually in retirement.

Let's travel back in time to the 1980s, when traditional pension plans were the norm for retirement savings. These plans were managed and funded by companies, providing a guaranteed source of income for retirees. However, in 1980, Congress passed a law that changed the landscape of retirement savings: the Revenue Act of 1978. This law included a then-little-known provision called section 401(k), which allowed employees to defer a part of their salary as "an elective deferral within a profit-sharing plan." Just like that, the 401(k) was born.

At the time, the 401(k) was not intended to replace traditional pensions, but rather to supplement them. It was a way for high-earning employees at companies to save even more towards retirement. However, what were Congress and Wall Street's motives behind pushing the 401(k)? What is the origin story of this whole idea? What makes it book-worthy? Here I need to set the scene with more context.

The 1980s Economy

The economy was suffering from high inflation, companies were looking for ways to cut costs, and traditional pensions were no longer sustainable. They required companies to contribute a significant amount of money towards their workers' retirements. This became too expensive. The 401(k) offered a way for companies to shift that responsibility onto their workers, saving them money and reducing their liability. Just like that, the 401(k) quickly gained popularity among companies as a cost-effective retirement solution.

Over time, as the popularity of the 401(k) grew, companies began favoring it over traditional pensions. As a result, it became the primary retirement vehicle for many Americans. While this provision may have started with good intentions, the 401(k) has since evolved into something entirely different, much to the detriment of many workers. The 401(k) was designed to be a part of a three-legged stool that included pension, Social Security Income (or SSI), and 401(k)s being the key to a successful retirement. Today, most pensions are gone, and SSI is about to implode. This leaves the last leg, the 401(k), as the only means for a successful retirement for many people.

Ted Benna, the inventor of the 401(k), believed at the time he was helping Americans with retirement because of higher taxes in the 1980s. But Benna does not promote the 401(k) anymore; instead, he calls it a monster he helped create. He would, "blow up the structure," per his words.

Source Marketplace https://indexedannuitysecrets.com/active-resources

Source Marketplace 2 https://indexedannuitysecrets.com/active-resources

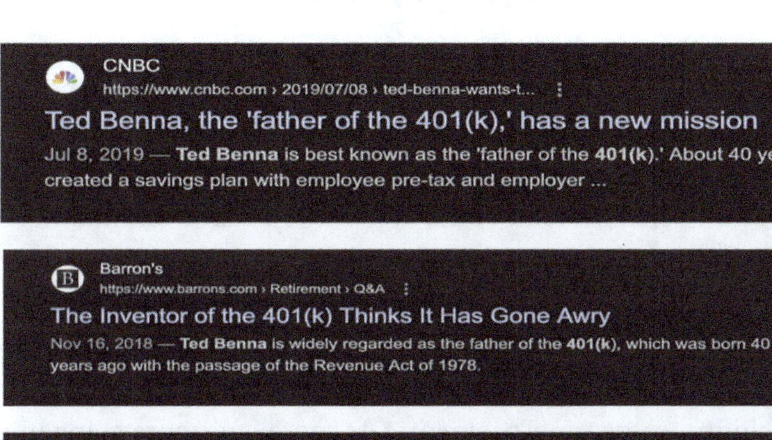

Wall Street and big business perverted the 401(k) in ways that even its creator couldn't predict. Our country is currently facing a retirement crisis that will continue to grow in the years to come because lifespans are increasing and 401(k)s are poorly managed. This means people are overpaying taxes and outliving their earnings because they're living longer.

At the time of writing of this book, the recommended age for retirement is 67.

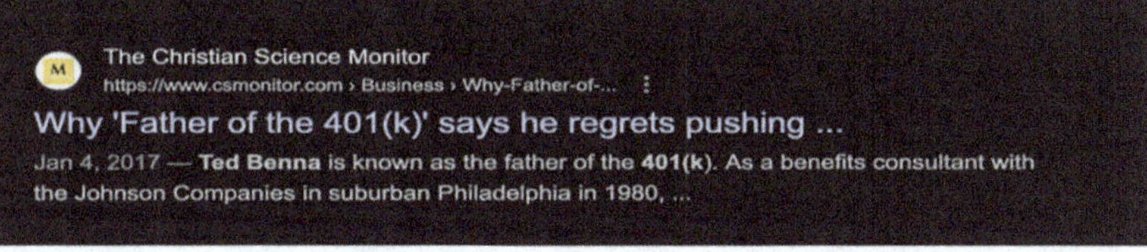

Source Nerdwallet https://indexedannuitysecrets.com/active-resources

In the following pages, I will dive deeper into the flaws and failures of the 401(k) system and the impact it has had on many Americans' retirements. It's time to uncover the truth about this retirement vehicle and understand why it may not be the best option for your future.

A Deeper Dive

It's time to take a deeper dive into the shift away from pensions. Let's go into the shortcomings of the 401(k). Throughout the years, the 401(k) has become increasingly popular as the primary retirement plans offered by companies. Why such a shift from traditional pension plans to 401(k)s? It's simple. As time went on, companies realized that 401(k)s were a cost-effective way to provide retirement benefits to all employees, without having to contribute much toward them. This allowed companies to save money and decrease their liability for pension payments. As more and more companies hopped on the 401(k) bandwagon, they began to tout it as the key to a secure retirement for their employees, pushed by Wall Street who lobbies Congress, who ultimately decides what we learn in schools.

With the promise of tax-deferred savings and potential investment growth, it seemed like a win-win situation for both companies and workers. However, the truth is that the 401(k) has not lived up to its promises. It has become clear that this retirement vehicle has some major flaws and problems that have left many Americans without the retirement they were promised. Unfortunately, many Americans aren't taught the basics when it comes to the 401(k). So, what exactly are these failures, and how have they affected people? Let's dive deeper into the flaws of the 401(k) system and understand why it has been deemed a failure for many individuals and families.

No Personalized Approach

Take a moment to reflect and ask yourself an honest question about your retirement and 401(k).

Have you ever personally spoken to the person managing your money?

Are they willing to take your call after hours or on the weekends?

Have they ever asked you your 5-year, 10-year, or 20-year goals?

Do they reach out and ask you how you are doing?

Have you ever heard their voice?

Have you shaken their hand?

You wouldn't hire a stranger to watch your kids after a ten-minute conversation, so why trust a stranger with your future retirement? So many times I see people place responsibility with the least amount of effort in this area, and I'm here to tell you it does make a difference.

There is something troubling with this industry. It has to do with bad products that are offered without education, combined with financial advisors who do not keep your goals at the forefront of decision making for your financial future. Do you imagine that rich folks in our society invest for retirement like this? In the next chapter, I will show you what the affluent do.

Why the Affluent Choose Indexed

Soon I will discuss the secrets of the affluent who already know how to protect their assets and retire safely. I will cover history, debunk myths, and explain many things while providing resources, real examples, and live accounts. A financial advisor could brush this book off and scoff at the idea of listening to this advice. They will offer a variable annuity or a fixed annuity with fees versus an indexed annuity with no fees or downside risk, and they will say it's only going to perform like a CD to persuade you away.

It's not their fault they work as a captive agent, meaning they can only offer what their company tells them to offer. This means they wouldn't steer you to the competition if they had a better offer.

The real question you should be asking your current advisor, if you have one, is whether they offer an indexed annuity plan, and how this program works. There are two reasons why they won't share. The first being that they don't know how it works, yet they have it on their financial shelves!

The second reason being that they know how it works, and they won't offer it because they can't make any management fees offering it. Remember financial advisors make money through a percentage of your portfolio, whether you make money or not.

Naturally they will only offer a program that benefits their pockets. I urge you to take serious consideration to what I'm about to teach you, as this can be the difference between hitting your goals or missing them completely. In the following chapters, I will show you how to adopt these principles into your finances to safely grow your money and one day retire with confidence.

Chapter 5

Tools Most People Haven't Heard Of

Throughout the years, I made a lot of investment decisions based on watching my own parents handle money. The actions they took when I was young impacted me later in life. In fact, they weren't always great. I watched them lose a lot in the markets, with property, and gambling in casinos or at horse races.

In 2008, I watched my father lose hundreds of thousands of dollars. This caused me to grow up avoiding dumb risks. This was due to seeing the suffering firsthand. I saw my family lose money in the market, then try quick stocks and get-rich-quick schemes and still lose. I remember being young and seeing our house was empty because my dad had sold all the furniture to get by for the month.

I would watch my father lose thousands of dollars and brush it off as nothing. It never made sense! That plan was never for me. I always wanted to take smart risks. I wanted guarantees. I followed a different plan than most. I followed the advice of the affluent, who say to never lose money. I followed this so much it has brought me to the success I experience today after a decade of applying what I teach.

I grew up knowing that trusting your job was never the right thing to do. I even had an avocado business as a kid growing up in Miami. It taught me a lot growing up summer after summer. This led me into starting my own business later on. I knew there was less overall risk as a business owner.

I had a hunch about not getting into massive setbacks. When I started to learn history as an adult almost a decade later, I realized that 2008 wasn't even the worst financial crisis in our history! The Great Depression was even more devastating.

I learned about tools in my research that are not widely known by the average adult, but the affluent are very aware of them. Yet another decade has passed, and I finally know and learned what the affluent use to build and guarantee wealth.

It's called investing with a legal reserve insurance company. A legal reserve insurance company is a life insurance company that maintains reserves at least equal to the minimum prescribed by law or regulation in the state in which it does business.

Between my wife and me, we save up to $60,000 a year with a Legal Reserve Insurance Company. Buying your dream house in Southern California isn't that easy in today's age. We do this because we know one thing, investing with a legal reserve insurance company gives us security so when the next 2008 happens we won't lose a dime.

It's mind blowing and an understatement to say most people don't know these accounts even exist. Before I proceed to the next chapters, I want to be clear and intentional to provide you with the same tools I use to help families gain a better picture, tools I wish I had had for myself earlier as I learned to understand our needs.

F.I.N.

The first thing I need to talk about is called a **Financial Independence Number, or FIN** for short. Finding your FIN is very simple but crucial. It involves calculating the age you will retire and how long you will be in retirement to find a monthly amount that'll be required to live the desired retirement.

Example 1- John, a veteran, is 41 years old, single, and lives in Florida. He served 20 years in the military and never had kids. Leaving the military, he found a new purpose in life and no longer wanted to work in the military or government. This made him ineligible to contribute further into his Thrift Savings Plan (which is a retirement plan for government employees). When we sat down, his main concern was that I wouldn't screw him over. He experienced some hard times while serving. His concerns were understandable. I will talk more about his solution later in this book.

John's goal is to retire at age 65 with $5,000 a month after pension and disability payments. He is expecting to live until 85 years old. He wants to receive $5,000 a month for 12 months for 20 years. John's FIN is **$1,200,000**. How did I come up with that? I take the monthly income amount ($5,000) and multiply it times how many months he plans to be retired (240 months), giving us $1,200,000. John didn't want the 40,40,40 scam. He didn't want to work 40 years for 40 hours a week to get only 40% of what he deserves.

Let's say he is to receive $60,000 a year before taxes in the state of California. After taxes, he will bring home an income of $46,347. That's $3,862 a month or 22% less than expected each month. In order for John to reach his desired monthly income of $5,000 a month after pension and disability, he will need to pull closer to $80,000 a year and be taxed $21,763.

Now if John wants to retire for 20 years he needs $1,600,000 in a 401(k) just to take $5,000 a month after taxes. Are you surprised? Anything less would not be John's FIN. What happens if John didn't plan? He worked his whole life and is planning to retire. Why should he sacrifice? John would have fallen for the 40 scam if

I didn't help him. I hope you are starting to see the problem. Most people don't plan to fail. They fail to plan. Did you know most people plan vacations more often per year than they do retirement?

Example 2- Sue the teacher is 44 years old, married, living in Colorado. She loves teaching kids, which she says is her passion. When I sat down with her, she shared she just had money sitting there with her job. She had no clue how to plan or what the numbers should look like. All she knows is that many of her retired co-workers are working at the local grocery store. She wants to retire at 65 with $5,000 a month, including her teachers' pension. She is expected to live until age 95. With the time she will have spent as a teacher, her expected pension is about $3,000 a month, which will equal $1,080,000 over 30 years. Let's find her FIN.

Let's do the math: **30 years x 12 months = 360 months. Then multiply 360 months x $5,000 a month = $1,800,000**. Minus the $1,080,000 covered in 30 years of pension payouts, this leaves a gap of $720,000 **after taxes**. Take a moment to reflect: after calculating your FIN, how confident are you on a scale of one to ten that your current plan will help you hit your FIN? It may take a moment.

Let's take a deeper look at Sue. For Sue to take $60,000 a year in Colorado with her pension included she will be taxed $13,106 and bring home $46,894 or $3,907 a month, which is 22% less than expected each month. For her to receive the $60,000 **after taxes**, she will need to withdraw closer to $80,000 from a 401(k) and pension to be taxed $19,946. This is where we find the gap: $36,000 plus $44,000 equals her FIN. To receive the $44,000 **after taxes** plus her $36,000 a year would place her at the total income of $80,000. For Sue to retire for 30 years taking $80,000 total and $44,000 from a 401(k), she would need $1,320,000 to cover the gap, paying $598,380 in taxes in total over 30 years!

Seriously, how many people do you know with $1,329,000 in a 401(k) excited to pay over $500,000 to Uncle Sam? It's a good thing I guided her to rollover her money into her Roth and contribute to her Roth Flexible Premium indexed annuity.

I will describe Sue's solution later in this book.

Questions I asked John and Sue

- What are your ten-year goals?
- What is your life goal?
- What is your reason?
- Do you want to own your house?
- Do you want to travel in retirement?
- How long do you want to be in retirement?
- Are taxes going up or going down?
- Have you worked this math out?
- Are you working with anyone?
- Are you crossing your fingers just hoping it will all work out?

These questions are nothing crazy; they are aimed at understanding the clients' goals further. It is what a good financial plan should look like. It will sometimes hurt.

You worked your whole life for a plan that doesn't even get you one tenth the amount you dreamed of. You have to set a flame under your seat. You have to see what many people have missed to see: to cross the finish line and stay retired you need a plan, you need help, and you need to take action.

The One-Page Plan

Here is the second tool I want to offer you. This one-page plan will serve as a resource for you. It is something I also give to our clients. Here is a link to a free PDF and a video explaining how to use it:

https://indexedannuitysecrets.com/one-page-plan

It's called the *One-Page Plan* and is used for building long-term wealth while comparing where you should be. I recommend you take ten minutes to answer all of the questions that I asked John and Sue.

Building wealth is easy. So easy, in fact, that it can fit on one page. Use the *One-Page Plan* to find your **FIN number**, **D.I.M.E number**, the **50/30/20 rule**, and your expected assets. This will bring you more clarity than 70% of Americans who believe they have a plan in place.

It could be complicated but it doesn't have to be

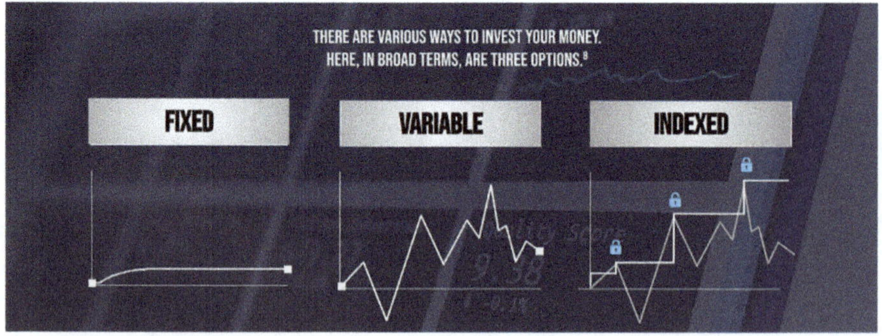

Indexed Annuity as a Solution

In the world of financial planning, indexed annuities have emerged as a popular and safe option over the decades for individuals seeking a balance between safety and growth potential. Navigating an indexed annuity involves understanding its features, benefits, and considerations to make informed decisions about incorporating it into your financial strategy. Keep in mind that not all annuities are built the same. It's important to understand which one you are purchasing and who you are working with. I hope you are ready and excited, but before I get started, here are some questions I like to ask people to get them to think about their current situation.

The Nuts and Bolts of an Indexed Annuity

Example with some of crediting around March 2023 to March 2024

STRATEGY	STARTING AMOUNT	RATE TYPE	CURRENT RATE	UNDERLYING INDEX % CHANGE	RATE OF INTEREST CREDITED	END OF TERM INTEREST CREDITED
AIPEX 1 YEAR	$150,000.00	PARTICIPATION RATE	120%	4.33%	5.19%	$7,785.00
BNP 1 YEAR	$150,000.00	PARTICIPATION RATE	145%	5.68%	8.28%	$12,420.00
NASDAQ 1 YEAR	$150,000.00	PARTICIPATION RATE	90%	45.23%	40.07%	$60,105.00

AIPEX - The AI Powered US Equity Index

BNP - Diverse range of assets across several geographic regions

NASDAQ - One of the three most-followed stock market indices in the United States.

PARTICIPATION - A percentage amount to earn

National Concern

I believe we have a serious problem in our country and that is a lack of financial literacy combined with advisors who over-complicate wealth management. We have financial concerns on a national level: inflation, debt, taxes, political cooperation, cost of living, and unemployment, just to name a few, are some things we have weighing on our shoulders at all times!

This doesn't even begin to scratch the surface when it comes to the list. However, it's important to understand that as I stated earlier, there are well-established companies and institutions that are safe havens for families, that time and time again perform well and come out on top against these tough circumstances. It's time to learn the secrets.

Legal Reserve Insurance Company Strength

You may ask yourself about the security of the life insurance industry and the companies offering annuities. To give you some context, it was as long ago as 1812 that the first U.S. annuity company, the Pennsylvania Company for Insurances on Lives and Granting Annuities, was incorporated. This institution came with a charter, or bank-like services, that allowed it to invest in other banks.

In 1929, a company called Wells Fargo surfaced after the Pennsylvania Company for Banking and Trust merged with **Bank of North America and Trust Company**. This is just a small example. There are more examples of companies that are thriving to this day, such as Penn Mutual and National Life, that have 175 years of experience and are well established.

In comparison, the 401(k), which has only existed for the last 48 years, has continuously failed the livelihood of many Americans. So why has there been such a dramatic shift from a guarantee to the uncertainty that is the 401(k)?

The life insurance industry has a solid track record of success for helping families achieve their financial goals for over a century, surpassing the typical lifespan of a business, which is now 21 years on average. *Below is an image on investing from a life insurance company's perspective.*

In this scenario, you give the company $1,000. The larger portion goes into the General Account supporting the Guarantees. Then the smaller portion goes into the options budget. This supports market-like returns.

Funding Methodology

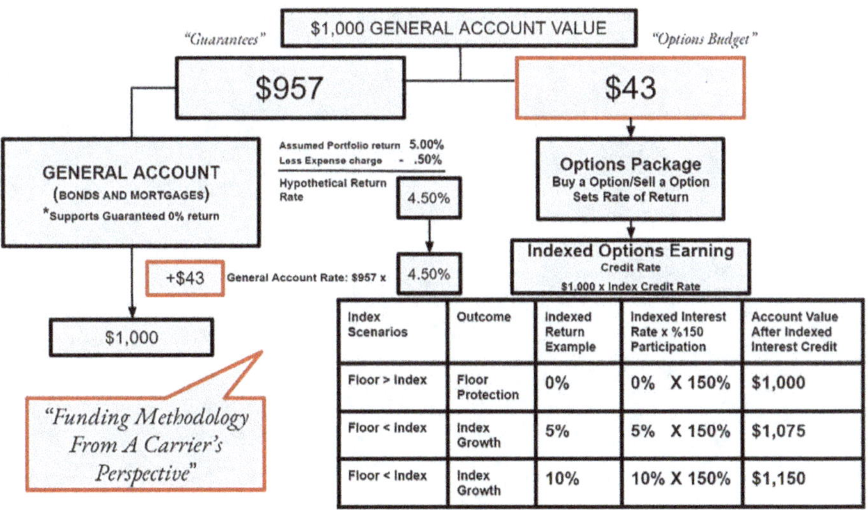

Index Scenarios	Outcome	Indexed Return Example	Indexed Interest Rate x %150 Participation	Account Value After Indexed Interest Credit
Floor > Index	Floor Protection	0%	0% X 150%	$1,000
Floor < Index	Index Growth	5%	5% X 150%	$1,075
Floor < Index	Index Growth	10%	10% X 150%	$1,150

Chapter 6

Fixed, Variable, Indexed

In this chapter I will introduce the solution, but let's start with a little knowledge. In the world of growing money there are three ways to grow your money. Annuities are no different: you can have a fixed, variable, or indexed strategy.

Ask yourself about all three of these strategies and how they work for your goals. As I've mentioned before, chances are you have only been offered fixed and variable options your whole life, including 401(k)s, CDs, Bank savings accounts, and so on.

What is fixed and what is variable? Fixed is like a bank account: if you earn 1% but inflation is 3%, it means most years you are losing to inflation and safely going broke. Variable is unpredictable, unreliable or uncertain. It's basically gambling.

Indexed is when the market goes up you go with it. When the market goes down you stay locked in. **In other words, indexed strategies are guaranteed never to lose principal.**

How come indexed strategies were never offered to you? Greedy Wall Street made sure you didn't learn about these secrets, because otherwise how would they get paid? They don't want you to guarantee your wealth for free. They don't want to help you do what's right for your family.

Here are the different types of annuities that 90% of people purchase.

Fixed annuity: A fixed annuity pays a fixed, set rate of interest, usually 3-4% a year. These usually come with a fee.

Variable annuities: The company invests your money — minus applicable charges — in a market account. Just like an IRA account.

Indexed annuities: With these annuities, your contributions are linked to the returns of one or more market indexes. No-fee indexed annuities also come with a guaranteed minimum payout when structured correctly, similar to a fixed annuity.

Immediate Annuities: These allow you to begin receiving payouts no later than one year after you contribute .

If I offer a fixed annuity, I can charge a percentage of the growth every year. These are glorified savings accounts at best. I've seen some so bad that the client was earning 2.5%, paying a 1.75% annual fee. If I offer a variable annuity, I can charge an annual fee called an advisor fee every year, regardless if it performs positive or not. Why not offer something better?

You can still lose in the market with a variable and pay the fee just like an IRA or 401(k). To give you a specific example, when I sat my own mother down, she had been investing into her 403(b) fixed Annuity for 28 years as a teacher and barely had over $35,000 at age 54.

The only difference between an IRA and a variable annuity is that the annuity is considered an insurance product. In other words, it's still in the stock market at risk, and the characteristics of the two are identical.

Financial advisors will place your money into a variable annuity inside an IRA and charge you fees while the market is crashing. That sounds like the only thing being helped is the financial advisor. This happens every day.

Average Versus Actual

Another thing advisors don't talk about is average versus actual rates of return. Let's use the picture below to show you further. Most people believe if you lose 50% and gain 50% you are breaking even. Here is the real answer: you are losing money and an advisor will trick you by saying your average rate of return was even. They simply add the percentage and divide by the years. Four years divided by a 100% gain and 100% loss will on paper equal 0% average over four years. Let's make sure to simplify:

- Starting at $100,000,
- Losing 50% places you at $50,000.
- Then when you come up 50%, you only gained 50% of $50,000,
- Which is $25,000, putting your new total at $75,000.
- **After repeating this process twice, you lose $43,750.**
- Going down 50%, up 50%, down 50%, and back up again 50%
- **Would translate to an average rate of return of 0%.**
- But the actual case is you lost **$43,750 (See image below)**

An Example of Average vs. Actual

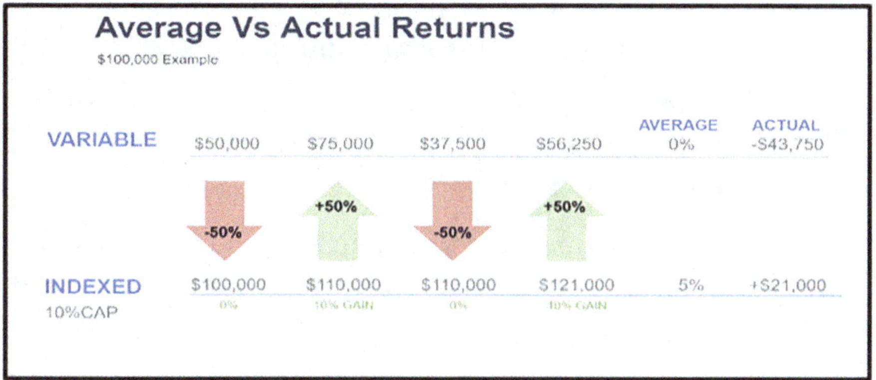

As you can see, this is very misleading. I was shocked to learn that most people don't even track their retirement this far. They simply trust their job to handle it. Using an indexed annuity approach, you can have actual rates of return of 5% or $21,000 over four years, being able to capture actual returns.

Annuity is its ability to protect the principal amount and still earn market-like returns. Indexed annuities guarantee that your initial investment is safe from market crashes.

Indexed Interest Credits: an indexed annuity offers the opportunity to earn interest based on the performance of an index with a monthly or annual point-to-point approach.

Uncapped Returns, Floors, and Participation Rates: Companies offer uncapped returns, floors, and participation rates on the interest credited. Uncapped returns offer market-like gains, floors set a guarantee to never suffer a loss in a down year, while participation rates determine what percentage of the index's gains will be credited to your indexed annuity.

Tax-Deferred Growth: Like other types of accounts, indexed annuities offer tax-deferred growth, meaning you don't pay taxes on earnings until you make withdrawals.

Income Stream in Retirement: indexed annuities can be structured to provide a steady income stream during retirement.

No Contribution Limits: Unlike retirement accounts such as IRAs and 401(k)s, flexible premium indexed annuities do not have contribution limits.

No Fees and Charges: indexed annuities can often come with no fees or charges. They can come with fees, with optional riders, or benefits.

The 0% Floor Is Your Hero

Growth Example

The following graph is an example of a "growth" indexed annuity with a 0% floor: your money is in an indexed annuity versus a regular IRA/401(k).

These are used to grow aggressively.

I followed a historical rate of return from 1998 to 2022.

As you read these graphs in the story, here are a few things I want to explain.

- First you look at the year (top left)
- Then you look at the money placed into the program in that year under **"Annual outlay year"** (each line represents each year through the market).
- Keep an eye on what **"Weighted average underlying index"** does and compare **"variable market"** (yellow) against **"Indexed point to point with 0% floor"** (green).
- When the market goes up, so does the indexed annuity.
- When the market goes down, a **"0% floor"** exists for protection.
- Follow each side every year and watch the compounding happen.
- Ask yourself: after 25 years, where would you rather be?

Terms:

Annual Outlay year: Money invested

Weighted Average Underlying Index: Annual rate of return

Variable market: The stock market

Indexed point to point: Following the market participating in the upside, never losing in the downside.

0% floor: Never lose principal protection feature.

STOCK YEAR	ANNUAL OUTLAY YEAR	WEIGHTED AVG. UNDERLYING INDEX	VARIABLE MARKET	CREDITING PERCENTAGE	INDEXED POINT TO POINT WITH 0% FLOOR
1998	$250,000	26.67%	$316,675.00	26.67%	$316,675.00
1999	0	19.53%	$378,521.62	19.53%	$378,521.62
2000	0	-12.66%	$330,600.78	0%	$378,521.62
2001	0	-10.53%	$295,788.51	0%	$378,521.62
2002	0	-23.37%	$226,662.73	0%	$378,521.62
2003	0	26.38%	$286,456.35	26.38%	$478,375.62
2004	0	8.99%	$312,208.77	8.99%	$521,381.58
2005	0	4.69%	$326,851.36	4.69%	$545,834.37
2006	0	11.65%	$364,929.54	11.65%	$609,424.07
2007	0	3.63%	$378,176.48	3.63%	$631,546.16
2008	0	-38.49%	$232,616.35	0%	$631,546.16
2009	0	23.45%	$287,164.88	23.45%	$779,643.73
2010	0	12.78%	$323,864.55	12.78%	$879,282.19
2011	0	1.54%	$328,852.06	1.54%	$892,823.13
2012	0	11.68%	$367,267.98	11.68%	$997,104.87
2013	0	29.6%	$475,971.52	29.6%	$1,292,247.91
2014	0	11.39%	$530,184.67	11.39%	$1,439,434.94
2015	0	-0.73%	$526,321.32	0%	$1,439,434.94
2016	0	10.46%	$581,366.79	10.46%	$1,589,999.83
2017	0	19.4%	$694,151.94	19.4%	$1,898,459.79
2018	0	-7.01%	$654,491.88	0%	$1,898,459.79
2019	0	28.88%	$831,909.93	28.88%	$2,446,734.97
2020	0	16.26%	$967,178.48	16.26%	$2,844,574.07
2021	0	26.89%	$1,227,252.77	26.89%	$3,609,480.03
2022	0	-22.9%	$946,211.88	0%	$3,609,480.03

This is a hypothetical example based on historical averages and assumes specific index performance. Actual results will vary. Consult a financial professional for personalized projections.

"But Can I Get a Better Return?"

You might think the point of this section is to try and convince you that you can't get better returns, but it's not. Remember what I said in the beginning?

I strongly believe that other forms of investing will fall very short of an indexed annuity in any ten-year period with far less risk, especially stocks and mutual funds. The truth is it doesn't matter. If you feel you could get better returns somewhere else, you're willing to take the risk, and pay the fees, then an indexed annuity isn't for you.

That's fine. I offer education and knowledge, not high-pressure sales. What I want you to understand is that you only have one retirement, and would you rather risk your retirement or guarantee your retirement? Do you want to safely retire, or do you want risk as you approach 60? Look at it this way: your indexed annuity is creating a benchmark for lifetime income. You are locking in profits year to year. This will effectively lower your overall risk.

If you can guarantee a standard of living, lock that in as soon as possible! That's my personal advice. If you want to take extra money and risk it in the market, by all means do it. But don't tell me how you put 100% on black in the Wall Street casino and "hoped" to become financially independent.

There is smart risk and dumb risk. Which one is going to put your family in a better position? With an indexed annuity, the money is there for you to use in retirement year after year, so long as you are willing to take the smart risk.

The major difference between smart risk and dumb risk is simple. Ask yourself this question. In the worst-case scenario, are you still happy with your situation, or did you lose hair?

"The Fees Are Too High"

You may have heard some say that the fees are too high. Truthfully, there are annuity programs with fees. Variable annuities and fixed annuities have fees, **not indexed annuities**.

To reiterate. the programs being shared with you do not have fees. **No advisor fees, soft-dollar fees, or expense fees. There are no fees passed on to the client!** Any person who says there are fees to operate an indexed annuity is either uninformed or lying to sell a managed product.

In the indexed annuity world, the company doesn't pass that cost onto the policy owner. This is because the insurance company profits when you profit through the indexed strategy. Let me explain in detail. They may place your investment with a legal reserve insurance company. They place it into an account that earns a fixed 5%, then take that 5%, without touching your principal, and invest in upside options.

Upside options are like safety nets for investments. They let you benefit if things go well, but if they don't, you're not on the hook for losses beyond a certain point. It's a way to enjoy the good times without risking too much in the bad times. When those options that you choose one year later are up in the market, you make a profit. It's that simple. Legal reserve insurance. The company can't risk your investment because they have to hold federal legal reserves. It's federal and state law. Insurance companies have to disclose this.

They make a profit alongside you because they buy options at a discount. They do it with billions; they do it hourly. With that being said, they don't need to charge you because they make safe investments and earn billions every month with these option calls.

Social Security Will Be Around

What I am about to share with you is like the cherry on top. Most people don't anticipate relying on their social security entirely in retirement. They expect to supplement it somehow.

Let's break it down a bit. If you file your income tax return as an individual with a total income that's less than $25,000, you won't have to pay taxes on your Social Security benefits.

However, single filers that have a combined income of $25,000 to $34,000 must pay income taxes. Those taxes can be up to 50% of their Social Security benefits.

Unfortunately, despite doing your due diligence by saving your money and paying taxes in order to receive this social security money, there is still risk in your retirement years: the risk of it being taxed!

What Guarantees Do I Have?

Indexed annuity policies provide solid guarantees, more than a 401(k). Just read the contract. They have guarantees and non-guarantees. Your worst-case scenario still beats a 401(k) for retirement and lifetime income. Also, for the "guarantee" worst-case scenario to happen, the market would have to crash and suffer year after year for the rest of your life. This has never happened and will never happen.

Some of the companies that I have worked with recommend portfolio presets. These presets are better than any advisor can offer, as you are investing directly with a multibillion-dollar legal reserve insurance company. They offer U.S. and global markets.

The Safest Place on the Planet

In earlier chapters, I discussed the time of the Great Depression, a profound moment in history. Despite this era's widespread chaos and confusion, legal reserve insurance companies remained steadfast. While I can offer no absolute assurance against unforeseen events, the historical evidence suggests that legal reserve insurance companies are the optimal choice for safeguarding capital. This is why banks rely so heavily on them. For more than over a century, they have consistently shown growth.

The Death Benefit and Long-Term Care

First and foremost, it's vital to grasp that the insurance company now offers benefits that include your long-term care bill, ensuring financial protection for you and your loved ones. If your money is growing securely while also providing long-term care insurance coverage, it's an obvious choice.

The question then becomes, "How does this work?" Having an indexed annuity with Activities of Daily Living (ADL) protection is a significant advantage of these policies. In other words, if you can't perform two out of six daily living activities, they pay a death benefit to you for your long-term care costs. This is a form of **guaranteed income** that you can use for long-term care if needed or other expenses in retirement. You might unwittingly leave a burden to your loved ones without this type of planning.

Another crucial point to consider is the continuous increase in the death benefit. As the account value accumulates within your policy, the death benefit naturally rises.

The more value you build into the policy, the higher the death benefit. Therefore, as you age, you'll build more money for your long-term care bill or your family legacy.

Can you see yet why this book is so powerful?

PART III
THE SECRET

Chapter 7

Betty, Sue, John and Rob

So far in this book, I have explored the failures and shortcomings of the 401(k). I have explained the myths and common mistakes that I see people make.

It's time to introduce you to the solution that I offered to Betty, Sue, John, and Rob. Although their names are changed, rest assured these are real people whose real dilemmas I have helped to solve.

In chapters seven and eight, I have shown four different scenarios. None of these scenarios are a guarantee, but instead they are only a look into what could be possible.

- Betty (age 63) did a **rollover** in an **indexed annuity**.
- Sue (age 44) did a **Roth rollover** and contribution in an **indexed annuity**.
- Rob (age 58) did a **rollover** into an **indexed annuity** with withdrawals for tax-free money into **cash value life insurance**, including long-term care.
- John (age 41) did a **rollover** in an **indexed annuity** with withdrawals for tax-free money under 72(t) into **cash value life insurance** for retirement.

In these next chapters, I am going to break down the indexed annuity program further and the four strategies that I see commonly used with the indexed annuity program.

Further Context

Scenario one: Betty's problem was terrible financial advice alongside no roadmap or plan. *Betty's solution* is a $900,000 rollover from her 401(k) into a growth-focused indexed annuity with a 10% bonus. It has no cost associated with the program, and it will pay Betty $100,000 every year as long as she lives starting at age 70.

Scenario two: Sue's problem was that teachers and schools don't provide any outside resources for retirement. *Sue's solution* is a $12,200 Roth rollover from her 403(b) into a flexible premium indexed annuity with a $300-a-month contribution. This program is designed for growth and has no cost associated with the program.

Scenario three: Rob's problem was a financial advisor who was more concerned with charging Rob fees than actually growing and managing his money. *Rob's solution* is a $300,000 rollover from his IRA into an indexed annuity. He makes $16,000 withdrawals annually at age 59 ½ into cash value life insurance and is planning to turn on lifetime income at 75. He also included long-term care in his program.

Scenario four: John's problem was not having anyone coach him with a roadmap. It's hard to trust when the military gives no information for 20 years. *John's solution* is a $160,000 rollover from his Thrift Savings Plan into an indexed annuity while taking $11,000 through 72(t) withdrawals and placing them into cash value life insurance.

- **TSP** - Thrift Savings Plan for government workers
- **72(t) is a tax code** that allows you to pull out of 401(k) and avoid the 10% early withdrawal penalty
- **403(b)** Teachers' version of a 401(k)

Betty was 63 when I helped her do a rollover out of her IRA into the indexed annuity from her financial advisor. By doing a rollover, I avoided any taxes and penalties and will wait for tax-later income at her expected retirement age of 70.

Sue was 44 and didn't have enough for retirement, as she is still fairly young in her teaching career. I helped her learn about her teachers' pension and educated her on the gap not being spoken about. She started with a small account and continues to grow her tax free account inside her flexible premium indexed annuity design.

I was able to help **Rob** who was 58 and **John** who was 41 using rollovers with withdrawals to a cash value life insurance policy and will discuss their details in this upcoming chapter.

All of my clients loved these options, especially when I took the time needed to explain how it works and be thorough. They all got peace of mind, they all saved more, they all acted, and all will be happy for years to come.

The average client I have will spend about six to ten hours learning and being educated on retirement before moving forward.

Betty Rolled Over $900,000

There is no minimum or maximum when starting an indexed annuity.

You can start with $100 or you can start with $10,000,000. Betty just happened to have $900,000 when I helped her set up her indexed annuity.

When Betty at age 63 rolled over her money, on day one she received a 10% bonus of $90,000. In her first year, she had a return of over $100,000. She received a rate of return in the market that was an effective 22.22% return. She loved the idea of growth and protection.

By the time Betty turns 75, she will have over $2,000,000 in her indexed annuity, just by assuming what the market has already done.

- She would turn $900,000 into $2,016,303.53 in the indexed annuity in 12 years. This is very conservative.
- She will hit her FIN.
- Her plan is to retire at age 70

If she turns on income at age 70 and takes $100,000 a year, conservatively she will pull out $2,000,000 by age 90. Not too bad for a $900,000 rollover.

By setting up this plan with Betty she will hit her goals. Betty can look her children in the eyes and with confidence let them know that they don't have to worry about her financially. Ultimately that's what it all boils down to: being able to secure her future income and provide with clarity.

Betty's $900,000 rollover into a indexed annuity

AGE	ANNUAL OUTLAY	BONUS APPLIED	AVERAGE UNDERLYING INDEX %	CREDITING PERCENTAGE	TOTAL ACCUMULATION VALUE
63	$900,000.00	$90,000.00	22.22%	$110,023.59	$1,100,023.59
64	$0.00	$0.00	0.56%	$6,121.56	$1,106,145.15
65	$0.00	$0.00	5.20%	$57,523.67	$1,163,668.82
66	$0.00	$0.00	12.05%	$140,269.81	$1,303,938.63
67	$0.00	$0.00	0.77%	$10,018.78	$1,313,957.41
68	$0.00	$0.00	12.02%	$157,958.19	$1,471,915.60
69	$0.00	$0.00	6.80%	$100,080.58	$1,571,996.18
70	$0.00	$0.00	4.00%	$62,952.77	$1,634,948.95
71	$0.00	$0.00	0.25%	$4,155.56	$1,639,104.51
72	$0.00	$0.00	3.96%	$64,974.86	$1,704,079.37
73	$0.00	$0.00	11.73%	$199,862.10	$1,903,941.47
74	$0.00	$0.00	0.53%	$10,064.39	$1,914,005.86
75	$0.00	$0.00	5.34%	$102,297.67	$2,016,303.53
76	$0.00	$0.00	12.17%	$245,336.35	$2,261,639.88
77	$0.00	$0.00	0.79%	$17,878.38	$2,279,518.26
78	$0.00	$0.00	12.34%	$281,181.29	$2,560,699.55
79	$0.00	$0.00	7.37%	$188,813.42	$2,749,512.97
80	$0.00	$0.00	3.73%	$102,673.47	$2,852,186.44
81	$0.00	$0.00	0.20%	$5,721.79	$2,857,908.23
82	$0.00	$0.00	4.17%	$119,078.36	$2,976,986.59

This is a hypothetical example based on historical averages and assumes specific index performance. Actual results will vary. Consult a financial professional for personalized projections.

If Betty retired at age 70, taking $100,000 a year

AGE	ANNUAL OUTLAY	BONUS APPLIED	ANNUALIZED WITHDRAW	AVERAGE UNDERLYING INDEX %	CREDITING PERCENTAGE	TOTAL ACCUMULATION VALUE
63	$900,000.00	$90,000.00	$0.00	22.22%	$110,023.59	$1,100,023.59
64	$0.00	$0.00	$0.00	0.56%	$6,121.56	$1,106,145.15
65	$0.00	$0.00	$0.00	5.20%	$57,523.67	$1,163,668.82
66	$0.00	$0.00	$0.00	12.05%	$140,269.81	$1,303,938.63
67	$0.00	$0.00	$0.00	0.77%	$10,018.78	$1,313,957.41
68	$0.00	$0.00	$0.00	12.02%	$157,958.19	$1,471,915.60
69	$0.00	$0.00	$0.00	6.80%	$100,080.58	$1,571,996.18
70	$0.00	$0.00	$0.00	4.00%	$62,952.77	$1,634,948.95
71	$0.00	$0.00	$100,000.00	0.25%	$3,901.40	$1,538,850.35
72	$0.00	$0.00	$100,000.00	3.96%	$57,036.67	$1,495,887.02
73	$0.00	$0.00	$100,000.00	11.73%	$163,715.89	$1,559,602.91
74	$0.00	$0.00	$100,000.00	0.53%	$7,715.59	$1,467,318.50
75	$0.00	$0.00	$100,000.00	5.34%	$73,078.89	$1,440,397.39
76	$0.00	$0.00	$100,000.00	12.17%	$163,094.59	$1,503,491.98
77	$0.00	$0.00	$100,000.00	0.79%	$11,094.66	$1,414,586.64
78	$0.00	$0.00	$100,000.00	12.34%	$162,155.82	$1,476,742.46
79	$0.00	$0.00	$100,000.00	7.37%	$101,514.19	$1,478,256.65
80	$0.00	$0.00	$100,000.00	3.73%	$51,467.43	$1,429,724.08
81	$0.00	$0.00	$100,000.00	0.20%	$2,667.54	$1,332,391.62
82	$0.00	$0.00	$100,000.00	4.17%	$51,349.11	$1,283,740.73
83	$0.00	$0.00	$100,000.00	12.33%	$146,007.97	$1,329,748.70
84	$0.00	$0.00	$100,000.00	0.51%	$6,290.95	$1,236,039.65
85	$0.00	$0.00	$100,000.00	5.47%	$62,113.94	$1,198,153.59
86	$0.00	$0.00	$100,000.00	12.26%	$134,627.61	$1,232,781.20
87	$0.00	$0.00	$100,000.00	0.83%	$9,353.38	$1,142,134.58
88	$0.00	$0.00	$100,000.00	12.62%	$131,529.88	$1,173,664.46
89	$0.00	$0.00	$100,000.00	7.95%	$85,318.17	$1,158,982.63
90	$0.00	$0.00	$100,000.00	3.46%	$36,612.63	$1,095,595.26

Sweet Betty got some pretty sweet results!

This is a hypothetical example based on historical averages and assumes specific index performance.
Actual results will vary. Consult a financial professional for personalized projections.

Sue Rolled Over More than $12,200

Sue rolled over $12,200 with $300 monthly contributions into a flexible premium indexed annuity Roth account. She has some catching up to do, but she feels more confident after planning with me, using the one-page plan and knowing what she is planning for.

Sue, at the age of 44, rolled over $12,200 into her flexible premium indexed annuity Roth account with a $300-a-month contribution. By the time Sue turns 70, she will have done the following:

- Turn $12,200 into $349,544.01 in the indexed annuity by assuming what the market has already done.
- Grow it all tax free inside of the Roth.
- Have the indexed annuity provide protection from market loss.

Not too bad for a $12,200 rollover with an insurance company. I calculate that between 70 and 90, which is 20 years of retirement, Sue will pull out over $500,000 completely tax-free! She loved the idea of tax-free money and protection from market loss as a benefit. She's a teacher and spends a lot of time with her kids; I can see why she wanted help. Once I gave her the education she deserved as a teacher, she was a lot less worried because she could never lose money **guaranteed**.

I believe as I continue to help her year after year, she will outperform her peers compounding in her **flexible premium indexed annuity Roth account**. Using it will get her closer and closer to her dreams and goals.

Roth is a post-tax account similar to a 401(K), but the money going in has already been taxed and will come out tax-free.

Sue's $12,200 Rollover and Contributions

AGE	ANNUAL OUTLAY	AVERAGE UNDERLYING INDEX %	CREDITING AMOUNT	TOTAL ACCUMULATION VALUE
44-45	$15,800.00	12.17 %	$1,717.20	$17,517.20
45-46	$3,600.00	1.91 %	$370.84	$21,488.04
46-47	$3,600.00	5.35 %	$1,252.57	$26,340.61
47-48	$3,600.00	11.52 %	$3,256.36	$33,196.97
48-49	$3,600.00	3.36 %	$1,181.94	$37,978.91
49-50	$3,600.00	11.43 %	$4,558.30	$46,137.21
50-51	$3,600.00	7.52 %	$3,616.82	$53,354.03
51-52	$3,600.00	6.08 %	$3,360.81	$60,314.84
52-53	$3,600.00	0.88 %	$548.11	$64,462.95
53-54	$3,600.00	3.07 %	$2,039.56	$70,102.51
54-55	$3,600.00	10.89 %	$7,840.49	$81,543.00
55-56	$3,600.00	5.14 %	$4,286.98	$89,429.98
56-57	$3,600.00	5.26 %	$4,802.31	$97,832.29
57-58	$3,600.00	10.76 %	$10,732.51	$112,164.80
58-59	$3,600.00	4.59 %	$5,236.21	$121,001.01
59-60	$3,600.00	11.32 %	$13,913.40	$138,514.41
60-61	$3,600.00	8.02 %	$11,262.45	$153,376.86
61-62	$3,600.00	6.35 %	$9,865.39	$166,842.25
62-63	$3,600.00	0.94 %	$1,583.85	$172,026.10
63-64	$3,600.00	2.93 %	$5,093.98	$180,720.08
64-65	$3,600.00	11.21 %	$20,470.99	$204,791.07
65-66	$3,600.00	5.84 %	$12,076.88	$220,467.95
66-67	$3,600.00	5.42 %	$12,044.67	$236,112.62
67-68	$3,600.00	10.67 %	$25,401.38	$265,114.00
68-69	$3,600.00	4.84 %	$12,935.17	$281,649.17
69-70	$3,600.00	11.76 %	$33,345.10	$318,594.27
70-71	$3,600.00	8.53 %	$27,349.74	$349,544.01

This is a hypothetical example based on historical averages and assumes specific index performance. Actual results will vary. Consult a financial professional for personalized projections.

Sue's $29,000 Tax-Free Retirement

AGE	ANNUAL WITHDRAWAL	AVERAGE UNDERLYING INDEX %	CREDITING AMOUNT	TOTAL ACCUMULATION VALUE
71-72	$29,000.00	6.57 %	$21,074.75	$341,618.76
72-73	$29,000.00	1.04 %	$3,265.08	$315,883.84
73-74	$29,000.00	2.14 %	$6,139.53	$293,023.37
74-75	$29,000.00	10.16 %	$26,836.99	$290,860.36
75-76	$29,000.00	9.66 %	$25,301.81	$287,162.17
76-77	$29,000.00	5.27 %	$13,604.33	$271,766.50
77-78	$29,000.00	7.63 %	$18,526.81	$261,293.31
78-79	$29,000.00	7.76 %	$18,035.04	$250,328.35
79-80	$29,000.00	9.57 %	$21,172.74	$242,501.09
80-81	$29,000.00	9.49 %	$20,267.50	$233,768.59
81-82	$29,000.00	8.10 %	$16,583.29	$221,351.88
82-83	$29,000.00	2.76 %	$5,303.52	$197,655.40
83-84	$29,000.00	0.18 %	$306.38	$168,961.78
84-85	$29,000.00	6.62 %	$9,271.09	$149,232.87
85-86	$29,000.00	17.48 %	$21,012.04	$141,244.91
86-87	$29,000.00	1.33 %	$1,497.77	$113,742.68
87-88	$29,000.00	5.65 %	$4,790.01	$89,532.69
88-89	$29,000.00	15.01 %	$9,084.44	$69,617.13
89-90	$29,000.00	3.63 %	$1,473.31	$42,090.44

This is a hypothetical example based on historical averages and assumes specific index performance. Actual results will vary. Consult a financial professional for personalized projections.

Warning

It's likely you may feel a sense of empowerment at this point, and I strongly encourage you to learn from us and how I can serve you! It's not too good to be true; you just haven't heard about it yet! Visit us at **www.IndexedAnnuitySecrets.com** to take a serious step towards empowering yourself.

Roth Conversion

Throughout this book, we've exposed the cracks in traditional retirement plans like the 401(k)—from hidden fees to market risks—and shown how the affluent use smarter, safer strategies to secure their future. One such tool is a Roth Conversion, where you move funds from a traditional IRA or 401(k) to a Roth IRA, paying taxes upfront for tax-free growth and withdrawals in retirement. This approach is a game-changer if you expect higher taxes down the road or want to dodge Required Minimum Distributions (RMDs) that force withdrawals at age 73. By converting, you gain flexibility and shield your wealth from future tax hikes, but it's a move that demands careful planning with a financial professional to ensure it fits your unique goals.

While a Roth Conversion is a powerful option, it's not the only path to financial freedom. In the next chapter, we'll explore a transformative strategy that combines indexed annuities with cash value life insurance, leveraging the 72(t) tax code to build a tax-efficient, secure income stream. This "One Seed, Two Trees" approach, which has brought peace of mind to clients like Rob and John, offers principal protection and the confidence of never losing to market crashes. As you weigh tools like the Roth Conversion, prepare to discover this compelling alternative that could be the cornerstone of the retirement you've always dreamed of.

Chapter 8

Beating the S&P with 72(t)

The story in the following chapter will surprise you. Once you find out what is available, you will learn what is possible. A few years ago, someone in my industry referred me to two people. **They didn't know how to offer indexed annuities**, so they knew they needed to find someone to help. The first referral was an older gentleman who was in his late fifties whose name was Rob. The second was John, who was in his early forties. After a few conversations, both wanted my help and expertise to move assets into a "being your own banker" cash value life insurance policy from their TSP and Simple IRA. They'd read a very popular book I recommend.

The following chapter will break down everything I went over with Rob and John to show them why this was the best approach.

One Seed, Two Trees Approach

As they both approach retirement, securing a stable and tax-efficient income becomes paramount. Combining indexed annuities, leveraging tax-free buckets with cash value life insurance, and using 72(t) tax code can be extremely powerful. Imagine you plant one apple seed, and it gives you two apple trees! These strategies achieve security during retirement. This well-rounded approach combines the benefits of indexed annuities' growth potential, principal protection with tax-efficient withdrawals, combined with cash value life insurance provides a roadmap to a secure retirement. **Without investing another dollar.**

Understanding Index Annuities with 72(t)

The 72(t) tax code, also known as Substantially Equal Periodic Payments (SEPP), allows individuals to take early withdrawals from retirement accounts, such as IRAs, 401(k)s, or other qualified plans, without incurring the usual 10% early withdrawal penalty. This strategy involves taking equal distributions providing a tax-efficient way to access retirement funds before reaching age 59 ½.

These withdrawals are subject to ordinary income tax but can be strategically planned to minimize tax liabilities, especially when combined with tax-free income sources like cash value life insurance. More on that design soon. Indexed annuities offer opportunities to earn great returns based on performance, helping to hedge against inflation and preserve purchasing power with 72(t).

Reasons to Consider

Diversification of Income Sources: By combining indexed annuities with tax-free buckets through 72(t), individuals can create a diversified income stream during retirement, ensuring a more reliable income. **72(t) is a two-step process from tax-later to tax-free. Make sure to consult with a professional who understands it.**

Long-Term Financial Security: The combination of indexed annuities and tax-free buckets under 72(t) provides a foundation for long-term financial security in retirement. It allows individuals to access retirement funds efficiently, protect their principal, and maintain a tax-efficient income stream throughout retirement. Most professionals won't steer you towards this because of the liability of 72(t) if the client doesn't follow it to a tee. If they don't follow the IRS guidelines, the client owes all the taxes from all the years they avoided the EWP. It is crucial to understand that this is a strict rule.

How Rob Turned a $300,000 Rollover into a $50,000 Pension for Life

Rob at age 58 rolled over $300,000. He also received a no-cost lifetime income rider that starts at age 75. When Rob and I were going over options, he asked what else I had on my shelves. I educated him on taking $16,000 out every year until 75 and placing it into cash value life insurance.

Knowing Rob's situation, I knew as long as he was approved for a good health rating this would be suitable. He was very interested to understand this approach. Rob knows that he never has to worry ever again. He has guaranteed peace of mind and can sleep at night. He is very happy knowing he will never pay another fee and will never lose money in the market ever again. His principal is protected from market losses, offering stability unavailable in stocks. Rob, being over the age of 59 ½ when he started pulling from his indexed annuity, only paid the state and federal taxes on $16,000. He decided to invest the $16,000 into cash value life insurance. He loved the idea of tax-free money and protection with long-term care included as a benefit. By the time I applied for Rob, within one week, he was approved with a preferred health rating. On paper, he was healthier than me. By the time Rob was turning 75, in 16 years he did the following:

- Turned $300,000 into $396,059.57 in the indexed annuity.
- Grew an additional $359,831.00 tax free.
- The indexed annuity provides an annual tax-later income of $27,229.02
- The cash value life insurance would provide an annual tax-free income of $23,389.00.

This adds up to over $50,000 a year for the rest of his life as long as he lives. He also still leaves behind $195,126 as a death benefit by age 95. Not too bad for a $300,000 rollover with a legal reserve insurance company. I calculate that between 75 and 95, which is 20 years of retirement, Rob and his wife will pull out over $1,000,000. He will use this to take care of his family and travel to South America. He always talked with his wife about traveling in retirement and they loved the idea of Argentina in the summer and Brazil in the winter. Rob doesn't have to worry about any long-term care or running out of money. Note that these returns may be limited by caps, and surrender charges apply if withdrawn early.

See below for the cash value life insurance numbers.

See next page for Rob's Rollover into an indexed annuity with Withdrawals and Income for Life

Note: The Surrender value is the liquid amount it's possible to access

AGE	ANNUAL OUTLAY	ANNUALIZED WITHDRAW	AVERAGE UNDERLYING INDEX %	CREDITING PERCENTAGE	ACCUMULATED VALUE
58-59	$300,000.00	$0.00	11.61%	$34,825.44	$334,825.44
59-60	$0.00	$16,000.00	0.50%	$1,599.63	$320,425.07
60-61	$0.00	$16,000.00	5.30%	$16,130.10	$320,555.17
61-62	$0.00	$16,000.00	12.52%	$38,134.33	$342,689.50
62-63	$0.00	$16,000.00	0.74%	$2,403.65	$329,093.15
63-64	$0.00	$16,000.00	12.67%	$39,676.01	$352,769.16
64-65	$0.00	$16,000.00	7.04%	$23,711.09	$360,480.25
65-66	$0.00	$16,000.00	3.97%	$13,672.57	$358,152.82
66-67	$0.00	$16,000.00	0.18%	$620.77	$342,773.59
67-68	$0.00	$16,000.00	4.00%	$13,086.40	$339,859.99
68-69	$0.00	$16,000.00	12.45%	$40,327.29	$364,187.28
69-70	$0.00	$16,000.00	0.48%	$1,683.88	$349,871.16
70-71	$0.00	$16,000.00	5.46%	$18,214.43	$352,085.59
71-72	$0.00	$16,000.00	12.81%	$43,059.68	$379,145.27
72-73	$0.00	$16,000.00	0.78%	$2,838.52	$365,983.79
73-74	$0.00	$16,000.00	13.17%	$46,082.35	$396,066.14
74-75	$0.00	$16,000.00	7.73%	$29,392.77	$409,458.91
75-76	$0.00	$27,229.02	3.62%	$13,829.68	$396,059.57
76-77	$0.00	$27,229.02	0.13%	$480.31	$369,310.86
77-78	$0.00	$27,229.02	4.20%	$14,354.69	$356,436.53
78-79	$0.00	$27,229.02	13.28%	$43,706.93	$372,914.44
79-80	$0.00	$27,229.02	0.48%	$1,665.31	$347,350.73
80-81	$0.00	$27,229.02	5.58%	$17,873.37	$337,995.08
81-82	$0.00	$27,229.02	13.05%	$40,540.16	$351,306.22
82-83	$0.00	$27,229.02	0.85%	$2,743.91	$326,821.11
83-84	$0.00	$27,229.02	13.61%	$40,761.02	$340,353.11
84-85	$0.00	$27,229.02	8.43%	$26,401.07	$339,525.16
85-86	$0.00	$27,229.02	3.25%	$10,154.19	$322,450.33
86-87	$0.00	$27,229.02	0.09%	$270.65	$295,491.96
87-88	$0.00	$27,229.02	4.39%	$11,782.00	$280,044.94
88-89	$0.00	$27,229.02	14.07%	$35,573.29	$288,389.21
89-90	$0.00	$27,229.02	0.49%	$1,286.25	$262,446.44
90-91	$0.00	$27,229.02	5.68%	$13,367.68	$248,585.10
91-92	$0.00	$27,229.02	13.23%	$29,286.30	$250,642.38
92-93	$0.00	$27,229.02	0.93%	$2,068.24	$225,481.60
93-94	$0.00	$27,229.02	13.99%	$27,736.85	$225,989.43
94-95	$0.00	$27,229.02	9.12%	$18,126.84	$216,887.25
95-96	$0.00	$27,229.02	2.88%	$5,467.87	$195,126.10

This is a hypothetical example based on historical averages and assumes specific index performance. Actual results will vary. Consult a financial professional for personalized projections.

Rob's cash value life insurance Policy

AGE	ANNUALIZED PREMIUM IN	ANNUALIZED PREMIUM OUT	ACCUMULATED VALUE	SURRENDER VALUE	DEATH BENEFIT
59-60	$16,000	$0.00	$12,893	$5,761.00	$232,672.00
60-61	$16,000	$0.00	$26,409	$19,631.00	$246,188.00
61-62	$16,000	$0.00	$40,604	$34,195.00	$260,383.00
62-63	$16,000	$0.00	$55,522	$49,493.00	$275,301.00
63-64	$16,000	$0.00	$71,203	$65,568.00	$290,982.00
64-65	$16,000	$0.00	$87,908	$83,950.00	$307,687.00
65-66	$16,000	$0.00	$105,501	$102,259.00	$325,280.00
66-67	$16,000	$0.00	$124,008	$121,518.00	$343,787.00
67-68	$16,000	$0.00	$143,459	$141,758.00	$363,238.00
68-69	$16,000	$0.00	$163,880	$163,008.00	$383,659.00
69-70	$16,000	$0.00	$188,016	$188,016.00	$407,795.00
70-71	$16,000	$0.00	$213,363	$213,363.00	$433,142.00
71-72	$16,000	$0.00	$239,957	$239,957.00	$459,736.00
72-73	$16,000	$0.00	$267,828	$267,828.00	$487,607.00
73-74	$16,000	$0.00	$296,998	$296,998.00	$516,777.00
74-75	$16,000	$0.00	$327,481	$327,481.00	$547,260.00
75-76	$16,000	$0.00	$359,831	$359,831.00	$547,260.00
76-77	$0	$23,389.00	$375,386	$351,331.00	$523,205.00
77-78	$0	$23,389.00	$391,259	$341,874.00	$497,875.00
78-79	$0	$23,389.00	$407,509	$331,452.00	$471,202.00
79-80	$0	$23,389.00	$424,065	$319,921.00	$443,116.00
80-81	$0	$23,389.00	$441,317	$307,598.00	$413,541.00
81-82	$0	$23,389.00	$459,418	$294,558.00	$382,399.00
82-83	$0	$23,389.00	$478,598	$280,944.00	$349,606.00
83-84	$0	$23,389.00	$499,153	$266,969.00	$315,076.00
84-85	$0	$23,389.00	$523,368	$254,823.00	$280,991.00
85-86	$0	$23,389.00	$549,135	$242,302.00	$269,758.00
86-87	$0	$23,389.00	$575,538	$228,387.00	$257,164.00
87-88	$0	$23,389.00	$602,531	$212,927.00	$243,053.00
88-89	$0	$23,389.00	$630,049	$195,740.00	$227,243.00
89-90	$0	$23,389.00	$658,014	$176,632.00	$209,532.00
90-91	$0	$23,389.00	$686,357	$155,406.00	$189,724.00
91-92	$0	$23,389.00	$716,045	$132,899.00	$132,899.00
92-93	$0	$23,389.00	$747,372	$109,264.00	$109,264.00
93-94	$0	$23,389.00	$780,690	$84,707.00	$84,707.00
94-95	$0	$23,389.00	$816,427	$59,502.00	$59,502.00
95-96	$0	$23,389.00	$856,456	$35,359.00	$35,359.00

This is a hypothetical example based on historical averages and assumes specific index performance. Actual results will vary. Consult a financial professional for personalized projections.

How John Turned a $160,000 Tax-Later TSP into a $500,000 Tax-Free Cash Cow

John, at age 41, rolled over $160,000 from his TSP. He received a no-cost guaranteed lifetime income rider with his indexed annuity designed to start at age 65.

John left the military when he started "dripping" from his indexed annuity and only paid the state and federal taxes on $11,000 per year. He doesn't have to pay the 10% early withdrawal penalty under 72(t) and decided to invest that $11,000 into cash value life insurance. He loved the idea of tax-free money and protection with long-term care included as a benefit. He saw what veteran buddies had to deal with when getting no help. By the time I applied for John's cash value life insurance, he was approved within three weeks he was approved with a standard rating.

By the time John was turns 65 in 24 years, he will have:

- Turned $160,000 into $361,387.22 in the indexed annuity.
- Grown an additional $507,745.00 tax-free inside of the cash value life insurance.
- Have a pension which pays him $1,770 a month from serving his country and $1,660 due to his disability.
- He will own his house in Florida.

This adds up to over $800,000. John never had to worry because the programs are proven and John has peace of mind, which is priceless. He is currently traveling the world and living his dreams. He made me worry on how to make him money. Wouldn't that be amazing? Securing your future and getting peace of mind? Not too bad for a $160,000 rollover with a legal reserve insurance company. I calculate that between 65 and 95 which is 30 years of retirement John will pull out over $1,400,000.

John's Rollover with $11,000 annual withdraws under 72(t)

AGE	ANNUAL OUTLAY	ANNUALIZED WITHDRAW	AVERAGE UNDERLYING INDEX %	CREDITING PERCENTAGE	TOTAL ACCUMULATION VALUE
40-41	$160,000.00	$0.00	15.94%	$25,499.93	$185,499.93
41-42	$0.00	$11,000.00	0.74%	$1,294.97	$175,794.90
42-43	$0.00	$11,000.00	7.19%	$11,847.97	$176,642.87
43-44	$0.00	$11,000.00	16.63%	$27,551.46	$193,194.33
44-45	$0.00	$11,000.00	1.07%	$1,945.71	$184,140.04
45-46	$0.00	$11,000.00	17.58%	$30,430.43	$203,570.47
46-47	$0.00	$11,000.00	10.10%	$19,441.48	$212,011.95
47-48	$0.00	$11,000.00	5.39%	$10,843.21	$211,855.16
48-49	$0.00	$11,000.00	0.27%	$546.03	$201,401.19
49-50	$0.00	$11,000.00	6.17%	$11,738.40	$202,139.59
50-51	$0.00	$11,000.00	17.38%	$33,214.65	$224,354.24
51-52	$0.00	$11,000.00	0.71%	$1,507.30	$214,861.54
52-53	$0.00	$11,000.00	7.45%	$15,182.63	$219,044.17
53-54	$0.00	$11,000.00	17.15%	$35,686.88	$243,731.05
54-55	$0.00	$11,000.00	1.15%	$2,672.32	$235,403.37
55-56	$0.00	$11,000.00	18.36%	$41,200.44	$265,603.81
56-57	$0.00	$11,000.00	11.34%	$28,873.68	$283,477.49
57-58	$0.00	$11,000.00	4.76%	$12,976.40	$285,453.89
58-59	$0.00	$11,000.00	0.18%	$499.29	$274,953.18
59-60	$0.00	$11,000.00	6.46%	$17,062.46	$281,015.64
60-61	$0.00	$11,000.00	18.77%	$50,686.97	$320,702.61
61-62	$0.00	$11,000.00	0.70%	$2,179.76	$311,882.37
62-63	$0.00	$11,000.00	7.65%	$23,014.18	$323,896.55
63-64	$0.00	$11,000.00	17.57%	$54,972.53	$367,869.08
64-65	$0.00	$11,000.00	1.27%	$4,518.14	$361,387.22

This is a hypothetical example based on historical averages and assumes specific index performance. Actual results will vary. Consult a financial professional for personalized projections.

John's cash value life insurance

YEAR	AGE	ANNUALIZED PREMIUM	ACCUMULATED VALUE	SURRENDER VALUE	DEATH BENEFIT
1	41-42	$11,000.00	$9,370	$1,985	$363,720
2	42-43	$11,000.00	$19,261.00	$12,241.00	$373,611
3	43-44	$11,000.00	$29,711.00	$23,067.00	$384,061
4	44-45	$11,000.00	$40,756.00	$34,509.00	$395,106
5	45-46	$11,000.00	$52,434.00	$46,598.00	$406,784
6	46-47	$11,000.00	$65,005.00	$60,930.00	$419,355
7	47-48	$11,000.00	$78,347.00	$75,020.00	$432,697
8	48-49	$11,000.00	$92,498.00	$89,950.00	$446,848
9	49-50	$11,000.00	$107,500.00	$105,767.00	$461,850
10	50-51	$11,000.00	$123,396.00	$122,511.00	$477,746
11	51-52	$11,000.00	$141,673.00	$141,673.00	$496,023
12	52-53	$11,000.00	$161,037.00	$161,037.00	$515,387
13	53-54	$11,000.00	$181,558.00	$181,558.00	$535,908
14	54-55	$11,000.00	$203,303.00	$203,303.00	$557,653
15	55-56	$11,000.00	$226,351.00	$226,351.00	$580,701
16	56-57	$11,000.00	$250,798.00	$250,798.00	$605,148
17	57-58	$11,000.00	$276,738.00	$276,738.00	$631,088
18	58-59	$11,000.00	$304,267.00	$304,267.00	$658,617
19	59-60	$11,000.00	$333,483.00	$333,483.00	$687,833
20	60-61	$11,000.00	$364,483.00	$364,483.00	$718,833
21	61-62	$11,000.00	$397,270.00	$397,270.00	$751,620
22	62-63	$11,000.00	$432,001.00	$432,001.00	$786,351
23	63-64	$11,000.00	$468,750.00	$468,750.00	$823,100
24	64-65	$11,000.00	$507,745.00	$507,745.00	$862,095

This is a hypothetical example based on historical averages and assumes specific index performance. Actual results will vary. Consult a financial professional for personalized projections. 72(t) requires strict adherence to IRS rules. Deviations can result in a 10% penalty plus interest on all prior withdrawals. Work with a CPA or advisor experienced in this strategy.

In the following chapters, I am going to cover how you can take immediate action and a farewell message.

Chapter 9

The Road to Financial Freedom

When considering retirement options, the indexed annuities are very competitive. Make sure you have certain criteria when moving forward. Add this sentence: Roth IRAs offer tax-free growth, while taxable accounts provide flexibility, but lack the guarantees of indexed annuities.

I want you to use the one-page plan. Among other things, you should already have your fixed costs for retirement planned out, such as the cost of living and your expenses. Your budget should already be planned out, using the 50/30/20 method.

You also already know your true retirement age for SSI. Understand your life insurance needs and talk about long-term care so nothing can stop you. A bed in some long-term care facilities can cost $8,000 a month, and Medicare will not cover it. I want this plan to work alongside your other plans because there is not a one-size-fits-all approach. I want you to use cash value life insurance buckets to truly get powerful assets.

Using the indexed annuity will only provide peace of mind and help you fill the missing holes. If you are unsure about what this can look like having all the pieces together, I strongly recommend that you do more research. I will recommend a simple strategy call with me, and I won't charge you. Peace of mind is worth more. In this book, I can truly get you the retirement you deserve.

Taking the Next Steps with Care

It's concerning to witness the richest nation in the world grappling with financial struggles among its citizens. We seem to be living beyond our means, relying heavily on credit, and making questionable investment choices.

Over time, we've come to trust that the stock markets are the ultimate route to securing our future, that tying up funds in government schemes is prudent, and that financial advisors on Wall Street are infallible. In contrast, I trust that this book has succeeded in reconnecting you with our fundamental principles. Hopefully, it has illuminated the fact that one doesn't necessarily need to take risks to establish a robust, dependable financial base and that superior alternatives exist beyond conventional wisdom.

The indexed annuity emerges as a potent financial instrument capable of steering you back toward genuine prosperity. It has been a staple for ancient Romans, ministers, even earning the title "depression proof." The affluent American knows where to secure the future.

Despite being one of our most potent financial tools, indexed annuities remain widely misunderstood and underused by the average American. While not universally applicable, as not everyone may benefit equally, I firmly believe investing with legal reserve insurance companies presents the optimal foundation for financial strength. This strategy's benefits are unmatched, providing you with comprehensive control.

I have personally experienced deep satisfaction by implementing these strategies in my own life.

Thank you for dedicating your time to reading this book. My hope is that the insights shared here will prove as transformative for you as they have been for me. Chances are you have worked hard for retirement; I don't want to see you fall for the 40/40/40 scam where you work 40 years of your life, 40 hours a week, to get only 40% of what you deserve. Keep in mind if you don't type in the coordinates into your GPS, how can you truly get to your destination?

Allow this book to guide your decisions when switching jobs or careers, when planning 10 to 20 years away or more from retirement. Use it for a budget plan and having a conversation. Use this book when helping parents prepare for long-term care using indexed annuities with cash value life insurance.

Use it to help your kids understand what's out there for investing. Just remember that having choices is what allows us to truly get financially free.

At first, I wasn't going to write this book but then I remembered how Betty, Sue, John, and Rob felt freer after I served them. Sharing this book will save someone's retirement, dreams, and serve people. If this book serves just one person, then I have done my job here on earth. Enjoy.

Afterword

Financial expert Gregory Stevenson has helped thousands of individuals plan through the intentional training and licensing of professionals with the tools to offer an indexed annuity. If you are looking to become a licensed trained professional serving people from the comfort of your own home, email him at GregoryStevenson@IndexedAnnuitySecrets.com with the subject line **"Position."**

Many will benefit from our continued service. People who use an indexed annuity to build and protect their retirement will simply find financial peace of mind.

Learn more about him and his company by using the contact info below.

Contact Information

Gregory Stevenson: +1 (619) 374-8100 (a text will work)
LinkedIn: Gregory Stevenson
Instagram: Gregory_Stevenson

Website: https://indexedannuitysecrets.com
For the one-page plan:
https://indexedannuitysecrets.com/one-page-plan

The One-Page Plan

50% Needs /30% wants /20% invest BUDGET PLAN

INSURANCE NEED

AGE -

CHILDREN ($250,000 FOR EVERY CHILD UNDER 18) - ADD

DEBT - ADD

INCOME (INCOME x 10 YEARS)-

MORTGAGE/RENT- ADD

EDUCATION COST- ADD

TOTAL INSURABLE NEED FOR ASSET COVERAGE

SAVING MONTHLY -

TOTAL SAVINGS -

INVESTMENTS -

ASSETS -

EXPECTED ASSETS (AGE x INCOME /10) =

BIG WHY -

10-YEAR GOAL -

LIFE GOAL -

RETIREMENT AGE-

ANNUALLY/MONTHLY GOAL -

TOTAL F.I.N. AMOUNT-

NEED TO SAVE MONTHLY IN BANK -$________________

STARTING NOW

I should invest/save $_______ a year, in other words 20% of $_______ (annual income)

These are calculations after tithe (if applicable)

EXAMPLE 1

AGE- 31
CHILDREN- NONE
DEBT - $10K CREDIT CARDS
INCOME - $75,000
MORTGAGE/RENT- $1,500 RENT
EDUCATION- 0
INSURABLE NEED FOR ASSETS $760,000

SAVING MONTHLY- $500
TOTAL SAVINGS - $27,000
INVESTMENTS - $68,000
ASSETS - $6,000
EXPECTED ASSETS = $232,500

ARE YOU UNDER OR OVER THIS NUMBER?

BIG WHY - FINANCIAL FREEDOM
10-YEAR GOAL - BUY A HOUSE AND RETIRE EARLY
LIFE GOAL - SEE THE WORLD

RETIREMENT AGE- 62
ANNUALLY/MONTHLY - $7000 OR $84000 ANNUALLY
TOTAL F.I.N- $2,352,000 FOR RETIREMENT UNTIL 90
NEEDED TO SAVE MONTHLY IN BANK- $6,500 A MONTH,
STARTING NOW

Should invest/save $15,000 a year, in other words 20% of $75,000

These are calculations after tithe (if applicable)

EXAMPLE 2

Rick is 42 years old, married, and has two children. He makes $10,000 a month

50% Needs ($5,000)
30% Wants ($3,000)F
20% Invest ($2,000)
D- $290,000 Home (Current value $440,000)
I- $120,000
M- $1,800
E- $30,000
INSURABLE NEED- $2,020,000

SAVING MONTHLY- $1,000
TOTAL SAVINGS- $10,000
ASSETS- 401(K)- $160,000
Assets (should be $504,000) but is closer to $320,000 (EQUITY+401K+ SAVINGS) at age 42.

AGE x INCOME /10 = $504,000

John is behind the ball...

IF John is expected to retire at 60 for 25 years making $10,000 a month, John's FIN is $3,000,000 after taxes... Did that surprise you?

After notes for the one-page plan

If a financial professional recommended this book to you, **let them be your point of contact**. I'm not here to steal someone's client, but instead close the gap.

I show these examples because I am very often asked by my clients from 18 years old up to 75 years young, "Where do I invest, and how can I build wealth?" My plan is for everyone. My thesis is simple; it is built on guaranteed, smart risk, and proper budgeting.

From there, I focus on accumulation or distribution. I personally use the same tools about investing and saving that I teach to my clients.

Remember the goal is to save more and spend less. We have become so hooked on things that don't matter and lost the forest for the trees.

This tool isn't perfect but with some common sense and planning, it can be used to offer a road map.

People don't plan to fail; they fail to plan.

For a video going in depth on the one-page plan simply visit,
https://indexedannuitysecrets.com/one-page-plan
and I will email you a free PDF and provide a video on how to use it for yourself. ********

Contact Information

Gregory Stevenson: +1 (619) 374-8100 (a text will work)
LinkedIn: Gregory Stevenson
Instagram: Gregory_Stevenson

Website: https://indexedannuitysecrets.com
For the one-page plan:
https://indexedannuitysecrets.com/one-page-plan

A FREE GIFT FOR YOU

Get a Complimentary PDF copy of this book when you go through our website.

www.indexedannuitysecrets.com